A GUIDE TO
GARDENING BY
THE MOON

Michael Littlewood

Published by
Michael Littlewood
6 George & Crown Cottages
Church Street
Hinton St.George
Somerset TA17 8SD
© Michael Littlewood 2009

DISCLAIMER
Whilst every effort has been made to ensure that the
contents of this book are accurate and as up to date as
possible, neither the publisher nor the author can be held
responsible for any consequence arising from the use of
information contained herein. Neither can we be held
liable for any errors or omissions that may have occurred
in the book or for any work carried out by any individual
or company.

ISBN: 978-0-9563628-1-0

Edited by Gaby Bartai

Designed by Andrew Crane

CONTENTS

1 | INTRODUCTION

In this age and culture of houses with central heating, paved roads with streetlights, cars with air conditioning, and food from supermarkets, it is easy to forget to look up and acknowledge our relationship to the sun, the moon and the stars. Our dependence on the sun is obvious and straightforward: it gives us our days and nights, the warmth of the air, the light in our skies, and the turning of the seasons. Without it, plants would not be able to grow, and there would be no food for man or beast.

But also in the sky is another large celestial body, the moon, moving gently around the earth as the earth spins around the sun. It is a lump of almost inert rock 240,000 miles away, but without it we would not exist. The moon's gravitational pull acts as a check on the path of the earth's orbit around the sun, and without its stabilising effect the earth would face cataclysmic climate change that would make human life impossible.

The moon's gravitational force affects all that there is on earth. Its most obvious effect is on the tides, which reach their highest twice a month, on average a day after the full and new moons. Average rainfall also follows this rhythm, peaking three or four days after full and new moons. The earth's magnetic field pulsates to a monthly rhythm, becoming strongest on the days following a full moon. Laboratory experiments have shown that animals and plants are attuned to magnetic and electrical fields, and because all animals and plants consist of about 85 per cent water, they are also directly affected by the moon. So are people: more babies are born around full moon, police deploy extra staff, and psychiatric wards see more unrest in their patients.

Working in harmony with the cycles of the heavens has been part of mankind's wisdom and experience for centuries, and whole civilisations have based their agriculture around working with the moon, but much of modern gardening is undertaken without any awareness of it. Gardening with the moon appears in many guises and according to different traditions which have been passed down through the centuries, and over the past hundred years scientific research has established how lunar cycles affect plant metabolism and growth. By drawing on this marriage of ancient wisdom and modern science, we can start to work in harmony with all that is around us.

It is perfectly possible to garden satisfactorily without reference to the moon – but gardening takes on an extra dimension once you become aware of the cycles of the heavens to which plants are attuned. By taking account of these cycles when you make decisions about when to sow, cultivate and harvest, you can attune your gardening to them. The result will be a healthier, more productive, more rewarding garden.

2 | OLD TRADITIONS
The history of lunar gardening

Gardening by the moon dates back at least to classical times. The first surviving lunar agricultural manual, written by the Greek astronomer Hesiod, dates from the eighth century BC. Planting by the moon's phases was of great significance to Roman farmers, and various Roman writers, including Cato and Pliny, record lunar planting rules.

The Roman system focused on the differences between the effects of the waxing and waning moon. The underlying principle was that activities requiring growth or development were set in motion during the waxing phase, while anything that needed to dry or heal was undertaken in the

waning phase. Thus, sowing and planting were done during the waxing phase, and most harvesting, the felling of timber and the castration of animals during the waning phase.

The principles of lunar gardening spread across different cultures, and were transmitted down the ages. The result is a wide but disparate body of knowledge. Various different traditions have developed, and a new body of modern traditions has emerged. This accounts for the often conflicting advice in lunar gardening guides.

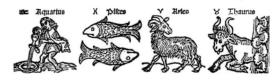

8 | HOW TO USE THE MOON CALENDAR

Planting by the moon involves taking account of a whole range of interlocking – and sometimes conflicting – cycles and events, and the first tool a prospective lunar gardener needs is a moon planting calendar. This will present all the information in an accessible visual format, noting the moon's position in the waxing/waning and ascending/descending cycles, its apogee and perigee, special events like nodes, eclipses and aspects, and whether the moon is in an earth, water, air or fire constellation.

The symbols used in planting calendars can be confusing at first, but they will become familiar with use. The information they convey will let you make an informed decision about what gardening tasks are most appropriate to the day – or whether gardening is appropriate at all. There are one or two days in every month where the influences are sufficiently negative that it is advised that you simply stay out of the garden.

Right: Sample page from Michael Littlewood's Gardening by the Moon Calendar, available from www.ecodesignscape.co.uk

OCTOBER

Date	Moon phase	Time	Crop type	Changeover time	Crop type	Saturn aspect	Time	Planting advice
1			E	5:00pm	R			✓
2			R		R			✓
3			R	7.50pm		♄	3.55pm	✓
4								✓
5				8.00pm	L			✓
6			L		L			✓
7	○	3.12am	L	7.25pm	E	♄	4.20pm	✓
8			E		E			✓
9			E	7.50pm	R	♄	5.00pm	
10			R		R			
11			R	11.10pm		♄	8.50pm	
12								
13								
14	◑	9.25am		7.00am	L			
15			L		L			
16			L	6.00pm	E	♄	3.10pm	
17			E		E			
18			E		E			
19			E	7.00am	R			
20			R		R			
21			R	7.50pm		♄	6.25pm	✗
22	●	5.14am						✗
23								✗
24				7.10pm	L	♄	6.10am	✓
25			L		L			✓
26	British Summer Time Ends		L	4.30pm	E	♄	3.50pm	✓
27			E		E			✓
28			E	11.10pm	R			✓
29	◐	9.25pm	R		R			✓
30			R		R			✓
31			R	3.55am		♄	3.50am	✓

Notes

EDIBLE GARDENING NATURALLY

● ◐ ○ ◑ ● ◑ E R ✦ ♃ ♄ ✓ ✗

The quantity of information can still be overwhelming, and it is useful simply to begin with observation. Refer to your calendar, take note of where the moon is in its various cycles and whether it is a root, leaf, flower or fruit/seed day, and observe how your plants respond to the different energy cycles. Then, when you are ready, start to put lunar gardening into practice. If it is a root day, plant potatoes, or thin carrots; if it is a leaf day, sow salad crops or transplant cabbages. If your gardening year is underway and your seeds are already in the ground, introduce gardening by the moon at whatever point your plants have reached; it will all be beneficial.

Once you become accustomed to this way of gardening, it is not difficult to accommodate the advice of a lunar planting calendar and tailor the work you do accordingly. It should be said, however, that moon gardening is not really compatible with sporadic gardening. If, for instance, you can only get into your garden at the weekend, it is going to be very difficult to schedule work with your crops for the appropriate time. Working with a lunar calendar is really only feasible if you are able to work in your garden at least every other day, so that you can undertake any necessary work with root, leaf, flower and fruit/seed crops within each nine-day cycle.

Moon gardening is also not compatible with disorganised gardening. Planning ahead is important; if, for example, you want to plant your potatoes at a particular time, it is essential that you have seed tubers, compost and tools to hand when the moon enters the earth sign closest to that date.

Work with potatoes should be undertaken on a root day. Picture: Dave Bevan

Be aware, however, that the advice offered in lunar planting guides is sometimes idealistic to the point of being impractical. For instance, one book suggests that in wet weather you should hoe in the morning in a fire or air sign when the moon is waning. This implies a period of some 17 consecutive days when hoeing is not advisable – which would result in a major weed problem. There are instances where the best time to do a job is when it needs doing, irrespective of the moon.

It is important to temper lunar planting with common sense, and to remember that a planting

2 | OLD TRADITIONS
The history of lunar gardening

Gardening by the moon dates back at least to classical times. The first surviving lunar agricultural manual, written by the Greek astronomer Hesiod, dates from the eighth century BC. Planting by the moon's phases was of great significance to Roman farmers, and various Roman writers, including Cato and Pliny, record lunar planting rules.

The Roman system focused on the differences between the effects of the waxing and waning moon. The underlying principle was that activities requiring growth or development were set in motion during the waxing phase, while anything that needed to dry or heal was undertaken in the

waning phase. Thus, sowing and planting were done during the waxing phase, and most harvesting, the felling of timber and the castration of animals during the waning phase.

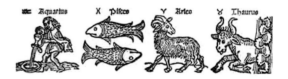

The principles of lunar gardening spread across different cultures, and were transmitted down the ages. The result is a wide but disparate body of knowledge. Various different traditions have developed, and a new body of modern traditions has emerged. This accounts for the often conflicting advice in lunar gardening guides.

3 | NEW TRADITIONS
Biodynamics

Concerns about agrochemical damage to the soil, the environment and human health have a longer history than you might imagine. In the 1920s a group of German farmers met to discuss the worrying decline in soil and animal fertility, which they attributed to intensive agriculture. These farmers were anthroposophists, followers of the movement founded by Austrian scientist and philosopher Rudolf Steiner, and it was to Steiner that they turned for advice. In 1924 he gave a landmark series of lectures which laid the foundations of a new approach to agriculture.

Rudolf Steiner

Anthroposophy (meaning 'the wisdom of human beings') is a philosophy which seeks to marry spirituality and science. Steiner advocated a middle way between the old world of folk wisdom and the new age of scientific and technical understanding.

He believed that such damage had been done by intensive farming that abandoning agrochemicals and returning to organic techniques would not be enough. Merely feeding the soil would not return it to fertility; the earth itself needed to be healed. To do this, one needed to harness all available forces, which included the rhythms and cycles of the cosmos. His underlying tenet was that everything is interconnected: a garden or farm is part of the wider environment, the earth and its ecosystem are a single living organism, and the planet is part of the cosmos.

Steiner's lectures formed the basis for the system of cultivation known as biodynamics, which builds upon the principles of organic gardening. It shares organic gardening's rejection of chemicals and its belief in the importance of building a healthy soil, and embraces many of its techniques, including composting, green manure crops and companion planting. However, it goes much further, adding spiritual and metaphysical dimensions to gardening.

According to this system, the key to healing the earth is to harness cosmic energies. One way of doing this is to work in harmony with the rhythms of the moon and the planets. Another is to use 'preparations', made from plants and animal manures and permeated with cosmic energies, as healing agents for the soil. The belief is that these energies transfer themselves to your plants; they will be healthier, more productive, and have greater vitality, and this life-force will be transferred to you when you eat the crops.

You can choose to garden by the moon without employing other aspects of biodynamic gardening. However, most researchers have found that planetary effects are only evident on land farmed organically, and are even more pronounced on biodynamically cultivated ground. Land treated with chemicals shows very little response to planetary influences, the implication being that chemicals desensitise it.

The Biodynamic Garden at Garden Organic Ryton, Warwickshire. Picture: Michael Littlewood

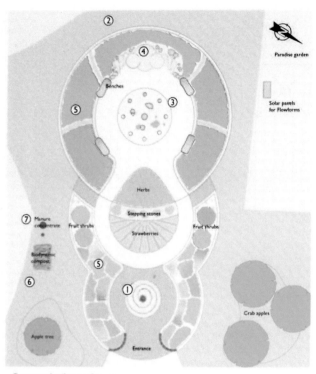

Features in the garden are:

1. The pebble spiral in the entrance represents the vortex created when stirring the preparations.
2. The main garden is surrounded by orbiting glass discs, representing the major celestial influences upon our earth (Sun, Moon, Venus, Mercury, Mars, Saturn & Jupiter). These are fixed within a petal shaped metal frame designed around the lotus flower.
3. The central island harbours the earth realm which is encircled by individual pebble mosaics showing the phases of the moon.
4. The Flowform water feature enlivens the garden by bringing in the active element of water. This rhythmical impulse transforms life and can be seen as the mediator for influences from the cosmos.
5. The flowers, vegetables and herbs in the raised beds are grown biodynamically and following a four year crop rotation.
6. The compost heap is treated with biodynamic preparations.
7. The manure concentrate pit is filled with a mixture of cow manure, basalt dust and finely ground eggshells. The compost preparations have been inserted into this mixture.

What is biodynamic gardening?

Biodynamic – bio (life) dynamic (force)

Biodynamics is a science of the life forces at work in nature and was devised by Rudolf Steiner in 1924, pre-dating organics by about twenty years. The effect of the sun, moon and planets reaches the plants in regular rhythms. Each contributes to the life, growth and form of the plant. By understanding the effect of each rhythm we can time our ground preparation, sowing, cultivation and harvesting to the advantage of the plants we are growing.

In biodynamics the plants are grouped according to which part you want to harvest - e.g. potatoes, carrots, onions, beetroot are roots; lettuces, spinach, cabbage are leaf; cauliflowers, nasturtiums, broccoli are flowers; tomatoes, peppers, strawberries are fruit. Planting the plants in these groups makes this much easier - roots on root days; leaf plants on leaf days; flowers on flower days; fruit on fruit days - using the biodynamic calendar to guide you.

Biodynamic gardening has a lot in common with organic gardening practices. Both reject the use of toxic chemicals on the land and believe in building a healthy soil, seeing it as the key to fertility.

Both use green manures, cover crops, regular cultivation, and composting, but biodynamics goes a step or two beyond organics, seeking to heal and nurture the earth through the use of nine plant based preparations which are applied to the soil, to the leaves of the plants and to the compost heap. These preparations and planting by the astronomical calendar are the main differences between biodynamics and organics.

Biodynamic Preparations

Preparation 500 (horn manure) – sprayed onto the earth.

Preparation 501 (horn silica) – sprayed onto plants at the four leaf stage, when the first fruits are being formed and again before harvesting.

Preparations 502 – 507 (compost preparations)

Preparation 508 (equisetum) – used to prevent fungal disease

More signs are located near the compost preparation area and elsewhere in the garden to explain these aspects in more detail.

A leaflet is available from reception in the shop

Garden Organic is the working name of Henry Doubleday Research Association. Registered Charity No. 298104

Display panel at The Biodynamic Garden at Garden Organic Ryton. Picture: Michael Littlewood

4 | COSMIC RHYTHMS

Plants are adapted to the natural cycles or rhythms of time – the day, the month and the year. The day and the year are solar cycles, and we are familiar and comfortable with the idea that plants are attuned to those. The month, however, is a lunar cycle, and its significance has been forgotten.

The most basic rhythm, with which our own lives are most in tune, is the daily one. Energy rises, or expands, in the morning with sunrise, and falls or contracts in the evening with sunset. In the morning, the forces of expansion cause the sap in plants to rise. In the evening, as the earth contracts, sap flows back down into the roots. It is therefore best to pick leafy vegetables and salads in the morning, when they are at their most succulent and vital. The evening is a better time to harvest root vegetables.

One can see the seasons as a similar cycle of expansion and contraction. From our perspective, the sun moves through an annual cycle, rising further to the east and higher in the sky each day from midwinter to midsummer, so that the days gradually lengthen. As the sun rises higher, the biodynamic approach envisages it drawing plants up from the earth. This phase of the year has an ascending force, dominated by the expansive principle of levity – the opposite of gravity.

After the summer solstice, the sun appears to rise gradually closer to the south-east and to drop lower in the sky each day, and the days shorten.

From midsummer to midwinter, we see descending, contracting forces in action. Crops ripen and bear fruit, then the remains of the plants are pulled back into the earth. Gravity reasserts itself as the earth contracts, drawing the sun's energy back into itself.

FULL MOON

WANING
GIBBOUS

WAXING
GIBBOUS

Rotation of Moon

LAST
QUARTER

EARTH

FIRST
QUARTER

Rotation of Earth

WANING
CRESCENT

WAXING
CRESCENT

NEW MOON

*Diagram showing how the light of the
sun falls on the moon, and the view we
see of it as it orbits the earth.*

SUN

5 | THE CYCLES OF THE MOON

The moon's cycles are monthly (the word 'month' derives from 'moon') – and it has not one but four. These describe its motion in relation to the sun, to the earth, to the plane in which the planets revolve, and to the stars. All have a duration of between 27 and 30 days, but none are synchronised, meaning that the overall picture is complex and constantly changing.

Put the whole picture together, however, and two patterns emerge. There are continuously ebbing and flowing rhythms of energy that the gardener can tap into. There are also specific celestial events which the gardener should know to take advantage of – or to avoid.

Waxing/waning cycle

The most obvious of the lunar cycles is that of the waxing and waning moon, referred to as the phase cycle or synodic month (from the Greek *synodos*, meaning 'meeting'). This is made up of four 'quarters', referred to as the first, second, third and fourth quarter. In diaries they are referred to as 'new moon', 'first quarter', 'full moon' and 'fourth quarter'.

What we see is the sun's reflected light on the moon as it makes its monthly orbit around the earth – a journey taking 29 days, 12 hours and 44 minutes. Because it reflects the sun's light from different angles as it moves, only part of the moon is illuminated for most of the month, and it appears to increase and decrease in size.

When it is new, the moon is positioned exactly between the earth and the sun, so the illuminated area of its surface is not visible to us. As it moves

around its orbit, it begins to reflect a crescent of sunlight, which gradually expands until the moon is seen from earth as an illuminated disc. At this point – full moon – it is on the opposite side of the earth to the sun. As the moon continues on its orbit, the illuminated area decreases again until it returns to its starting point.

When the crescent is growing, it is said to be waxing (from the Old English *weaxen*, to increase). When it is shrinking, it is waning (from *wanian*, to lessen). In the northern hemisphere, the crescent resembles a backwards 'C' when it is waxing and a 'C' when it is waning. A gibbous moon (from *gibbus*, Latin for hump) is greater than a half moon, but less than full.

There are two forces in play here which affect plants: light and gravity. Moonlight increases and decreases over the monthly phase cycle, peaking at full moon. Lunar gravitational pull has two peaks within this cycle, at new moon and again at full moon.

During the first quarter – the first seven days, beginning with the new moon – moonlight gradually increases, stimulating leaf growth. However, the moon's gravitational pull decreases, so the corresponding increase in the earth's gravity stimulates root growth. This is therefore a period of balanced growth. During the second quarter, lunar gravitational pull increases, so the earth's relative gravity reduces, slowing root growth. Moonlight, however, continues to increase, further stimulating leaf growth. This reaches a peak at full moon, when the night sky is up to ten times brighter than at new moon. The combination of maximal moonlight and lunar gravitational pull mean that optimal seed germination occurs at full moon.

During the third quarter, moonlight decreases, as does lunar gravitational pull. Leaf growth slows down, but root growth is stimulated again. During the final quarter, lunar gravitational pull increases again, so root growth slows down, and moonlight continues to decrease, further slowing leaf growth. This is therefore a rest period for plants before the cycle renews itself with the new moon.

As most plants do most of their growing in spring and summer, so much of the upward growth, germination of seeds, and creating of leaves and flowers, occurs during a waxing moon. As most plants produce fruit and seed in the autumn, and go through some form of 'death' for the winter, so much of the downward growth, creating roots and establishing plants, happens on a waning moon.

Ascending/descending cycle

The sun's cycle of ascent and descent is an annual one. The moon also ascends and descends, but over a period of 27 days, 7 hours and 43 minutes, known as the periodic lunar cycle. On one day each month the moon arcs highest across the sky, remaining above the horizon for the longest time; a fortnight later, it sinks to its lowest height above the horizon.

This effect is very latitude-dependent, and is more pronounced the further from the equator you

go; and wherever you are, winter moons are higher than summer ones. The ascending and descending phases are also known as 'running high' and 'running low', and can be seen as another manifestation of the expansion-contraction cycle (they are sometimes also called 'lunar spring' and 'lunar autumn').

Perigee and apogee

The moon's orbit around the earth is elliptical (slightly ovoid), so its distance from the earth varies. When it is at its closest point, it is said to be at its perigee (meaning 'nearest earth'), and when it is furthest away, it is at its apogee (meaning 'away from earth'). The cycle from one perigee to the next takes 27 days, 13 hours and 18 minutes.

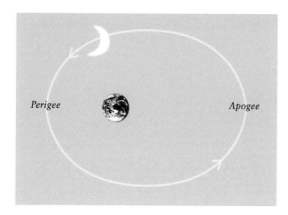

Perigee　　　　　　　　*Apogee*

The moon's gravitational pull – and therefore its effect on plants – is stronger the closer it is, and tides rise up to a third higher at perigee than at apogee. The moon's influence is strongest around the time of the perigee, and it is advisable to avoid all work in the garden on the day of the perigee itself. This is seen as a time of stress, when plant growth may be inhibited. Sowing around the apogee is said to make crops bolt, though potatoes do well if planted then.

Lunar nodes

The planets – including the earth – revolve around the sun in approximately the same plane, called the ecliptic, but the moon's orbit is tilted at an angle of 5°9' to the ecliptic. As it moves around the earth, the moon therefore crosses the ecliptic twice; once when it is ascending – the ascending or north node – and once when it is descending – the descending or south node. Disturbances occur when the moon is at its nodes, so these are unfavourable times for work in the garden.

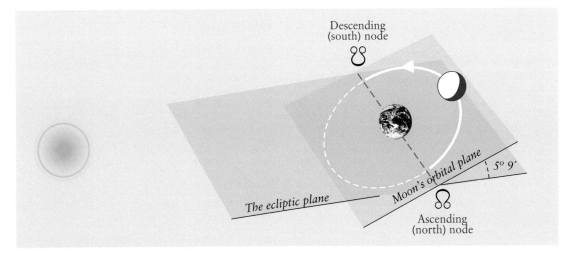

Descending (south) node

The ecliptic plane

Moon's orbital plane

5° 9'

Ascending (north) node

Eclipses

The plane in which the planets revolve is called 'ecliptic' because eclipses happen when the sun, moon and earth are in line on this plane. When a new moon occurs close to a node, there will be a solar eclipse, and when a full moon occurs close to a node, there will be a lunar eclipse. There is an ancient belief that the land is infertile around the time of an eclipse, and modern research has demonstrated that seed germination is inhibited at this time. Lunar calendars recommend not sowing or planting on the day of an eclipse; some advise avoiding the following days as well.

Planetary aspects

The angle between the moon and the sun, measured around the ecliptic and relative to the centre of the earth, is known as an aspect. At full moon, when the moon is on the opposite side of the earth from the sun, the sun and moon are said to be in opposition: this is an aspect of 180°. At new moon, when the moon is positioned between the earth and the sun, they are said to be in conjunction (an aspect of 0°). Other aspects are sextile (60°), square (90°) and trine (120°).

Conjunction, opposition and square are considered to be inhibiting and stressful, whereas the trine and sextile are thought to be beneficial. Positive planetary aspects promote the harmonisation of energy, leading to healthier growth, while negative ones can disrupt plant energies.

The moon also forms aspects with the other planets, and moon/Saturn aspects are seen to have particular significance. Saturn is traditionally viewed as important for agriculture, as it is thought to rule the structure of living organisms. Lunar gardening advice dating back to classical times views positive aspects between Saturn and the moon as particularly good for cultivation, and negative ones as particularly bad. Lunar calendars usually indicate moon/Saturn aspects, relevant moon/sun aspects, and other aspects of note.

Moonrise and moonset

It is generally recommended that an hour either side of moonrise or moonset is the best time to undertake any gardening tasks appropriate for that day, and these times will be indicated on a lunar calendar. The times of moonrise and moonset are especially significant if the moon is forming an important aspect on that day.

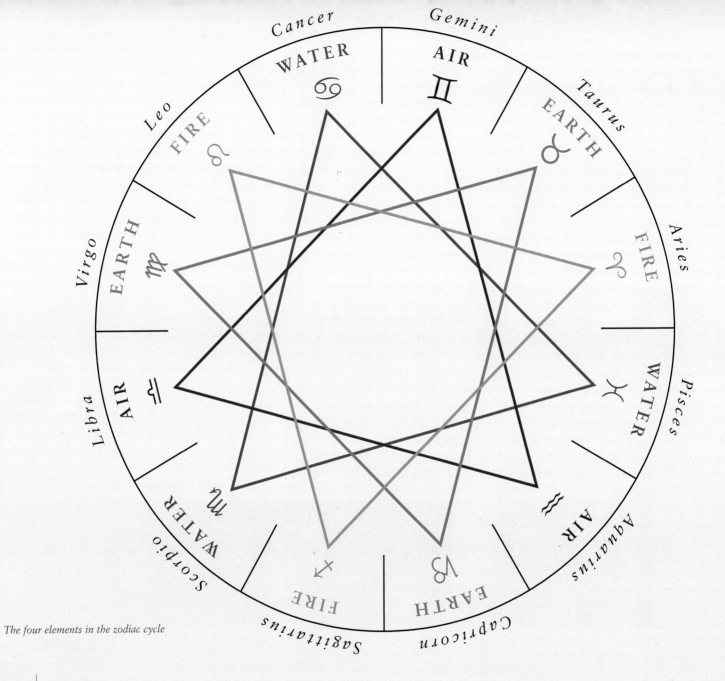

The four elements in the zodiac cycle

6 | THE MOON AND THE ZODIAC

Around the fifth century BC, the Chaldeans of Mesopotamia developed the idea of dividing the sky into twelve equal sectors, mirroring the division of their year into twelve 30-day months. Each sector was named for the principal constellation within it, and this gives us the zodiac, familiar to us from astrology.

The sun moves through the twelve constellations of the zodiac once every year, spending around 30 days in each. Because the plane of the moon's monthly orbit around the earth is close to that of the earth's orbit around the sun, it moves against the same background of constellations, spending two or three days in each.

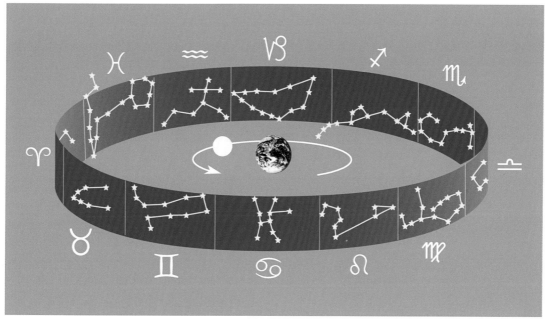

The sidereal cycle

(At perigee, the moon appears to be moving faster against the stars, so it takes only two days to pass through one constellation, whereas at apogee it takes almost three.) This cycle is known as the sidereal rhythm – from *sidera*, Latin for 'star'.

When the moon passes in front of, or 'through', a constellation, it activates the influences belonging to it and transmits them to us. If this seems far-fetched, remember that a similar principle underpins astrology. Though we have abandoned most other beliefs relating to the cycles of the heavens, the idea that our personalities are shaped by the constellation under which we were born remains firmly entrenched in popular culture. Lunar gardening simply extends the principle to plants.

The sidereal zodiac is composed of twelve 30° divisions, achieved by imposing a regular structure on the irregularly-sized constellations around the ecliptic. There are other systems; some lunar gardeners use the tropical zodiac, which forms the basis of modern-day astrology, while in biodynamic calendars the twelve divisions are of unequal lengths, reflecting the actual sizes of the constellations. However, most authorities, and the weight of evidence, agree that the sidereal zodiac is the best system to follow where plants are concerned.

Root, leaf, flower and fruit plants

In classical thought, four elements – earth, water, air and fire/warmth – were seen to underpin the physical and metaphysical worlds. These elements were linked to different parts of the body and used as aids in the diagnosis and treatment of illness. They were also associated with the four 'humours', or psychological states. In nature, they were seen to be reflected in weight, moisture, lightness and heat. In plants, they are represented by the root (earth), leaf (water), flower (air) and fruit/seed (fire/warmth).

In the second century AD, a link was established between these four elements and the zodiac. Each of the twelve constellations was seen to have a particular affinity with one element: Taurus, Virgo and Capricorn with earth; Cancer, Scorpio and Pisces with water; Gemini, Libra and Aquarius with air; and Aries, Leo and Sagittarius with fire. There are therefore four triads (or trigons) of zodiac signs, each associated with one of the elements. Because the moon spends two or three days in each constellation, it returns to the same element every nine days.

Steiner taught that there are four stages in plant growth – first the development of the roots, then the development of the leaves, then the plant flowers, and finally it fruits and sets seed. He saw each stage as being connected with one of the elements: earth works on a plant's roots, water on its leaves, air on its flowers, and fire/warmth on its fruits and seeds.

Root

Leaf

Flower

Fruit

In the 1950s, the German biodynamist Maria Thun began to develop this connection. She categorised plants as 'root', 'leaf', 'flower' and 'fruit' plants, according to which part of them we most value. Root plants, for instance, are those, like carrots and onions, which we grow for their underground parts. Her work suggests that if you work with plants on days when the moon is passing through a zodiac sign associated with the appropriate element, you will get better results, because growth on these days is concentrated in the most valued part of the plant.

If, for instance, you want to plant potatoes, you should do so on a day when the moon is passing through an earth sign. Planting cabbages should wait until the moon is passing through a water sign. Work with cauliflowers should be undertaken when the moon is in an air sign, and you should attend to tomatoes when it moves into a fire sign.

This principle relates to all work with plants, but particularly to sowing. The sidereal cycle relates principally to the instant when a seed is put into the ground. The theory is that the moon's position against the zodiac when the seed's DNA begins to duplicate determines how (all other things being equal) its potential will be realised – an idea which has echoes in astrology.

The assumption behind this principle is that the

Root days relate to the EARTH signs		♉ *Taurus*	♍ *Virgo*	♑ *Capricorn*
Leaf days relate to the WATER signs		♋ *Cancer*	♏ *Scorpio*	♓ *Pisces*
Flower days relate to the AIR signs		♊ *Gemini*	♎ *Libra*	♒ *Aquarius*
Fruit/seed days relate to the FIRE signs		♈ *Aries*	♌ *Leo*	♐ *Sagittarius*

Earth –
Root plants

beetroot
carrot
celeriac
garlic
horseradish
Jerusalem artichoke
kohlrabi
leek
mushroom
onion
parsnip
potato
radish
shallot
spring onion
swede
turnip

Water –
Leaf plants

asparagus
Brussels sprout
cabbage
celery
chicory
cress
endive
Florence fennel
grass
kale
lettuce
most herbs
mustard
rhubarb
rocket
spinach

Air –
Flower plants

broccoli
calabrese
cauliflower
edible flowers
elderflower
globe artichoke
ornamental flowers

Fire/warmth –
Fruit/seed plants

all berries
all fruit
all grains
all nuts
aubergine
broad bean
courgette
cucumber
French bean
marrow
pea
pepper
pumpkin
runner bean
squash
sweetcorn
tomato

seed begins to absorb water, and therefore to germinate, as soon as it is planted. It is therefore vital that seeds are planted in moist ground, and they should ideally be planted in the afternoon, so that the ground remains moist for the maximum period after sowing.

In trials conducted by Thun over many years, maximum yields in potatoes occurred in the rows planted when the moon was passing through an earth sign. The average yield was some 30 per cent greater from earth-sign plantings. Other studies have confirmed this. A comparative trial undertaken in 2007 at The Royal Botanic Gardens, Kew also showed a 30 per cent increase in the yield of crops sown in accordance with the sidereal cycle. The weight of evidence indicates that the yield of crops sown in healthy organic soil is related to the moon's position against the zodiac at the time of sowing.

7 | LUNAR GARDENING IN PRACTICE

Planting by the moon's phases

Plants' metabolic rate, their absorption of water and nutrients, their rate of growth and their electrical activity have all been observed to fluctuate over the cycle of the waxing and waning moon. Plants gain in vitality with increasing moonlight, and their resistance to pests and diseases increases as the full moon approaches. Their vigour decreases as the moon wanes – but colours, scents, tastes and nutritional and medicinal properties are more pronounced during this phase.

Sap rises during a waxing moon, and falls during a waning moon. As the moon waxes, water and nutrients are drawn upwards; this helps plants that produce their most valuable parts above ground, such as leaf crops, fruiting crops and flowers. When the moon wanes, water and nutrients move downwards, so this is a favourable time for root crops. This principle mirrors the daily rhythm of ascending and descending energy.

The best rate of germination is achieved just before a full moon. Trials by Dr Lilly Kolisko in the 1930s found that sowing two days before a full moon, compared to sowing two days before a new moon, resulted in better growth and larger harvests. Full-moon plants were juicier, and new-moon ones woodier.

The rationale behind this is that seeds absorb most water in the days before a full moon, when sap rises most strongly. A study at North-Western University, Illinois found that bean seeds absorbed on average 35 per cent more water just before a full moon than they did at new moon. Putting seeds into the ground two days before lunar forces reach their strongest point means that they will absorb the greatest amount of water, and the forces exerted on this water will create a 'tide' that helps to burst the seed coat.

However, other studies have suggested that the days immediately before a new moon are a better time to sow, so that germinating seeds can take advantage of the increasing and upward forces of the waxing moon. This system advises planting long-germinating seeds in the third quarter, and short- and extra-long-germinating seeds in the fourth quarter, so that all are ready to germinate around the time of the new moon. (Extra-long-germinating seeds are defined as those that take a month to germinate, so they will germinate at the time of the next new moon.)

Following the principle that sap rises on a waxing moon and falls on a waning moon, grafting should be done during a waxing moon because rising sap will help the graft to establish, and pruning should be done on a waning moon, so that cut surfaces heal quickly. Some authorities recommend transplanting under a waxing moon, but others argue that the third quarter is better, because this phase favours root growth, resulting in better establishment.

You should dig and add manure or compost to the soil at the start of the moon's fourth quarter. As the water table recedes over the course of the fourth quarter, it releases pressure on the soil and encourages a more thorough and deeper absorption of additives. If organic matter is applied at the correct moon time, it can be reduced by as much as 50 per cent of the recommended quantity.

The water cycle linked to the waxing and waning moon also has implications for harvesting. Plants harvested around the time of a full moon are said to have most vitality, so this is the best time to pick crops that will be eaten quickly. Crops that are

From 'How to Grow More Vegetables' by John Jeavons

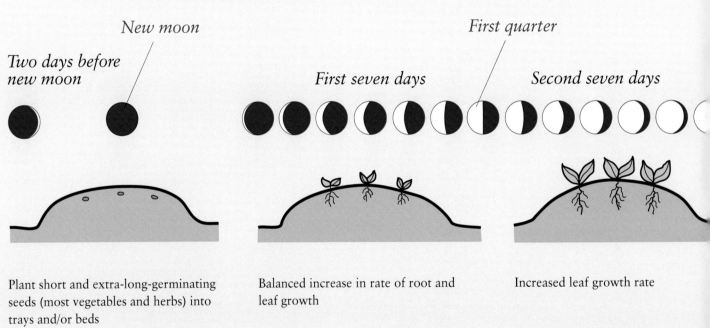

New moon

Two days before new moon

First quarter

First seven days

Second seven days

Plant short and extra-long-germinating seeds (most vegetables and herbs) into trays and/or beds

Balanced increase in rate of root and leaf growth

Increased leaf growth rate

MOONLIGHT INCREASING
LUNAR GRAVITY DECREASING

MOONLIGHT INCREASING
LUNAR GRAVITY INCREASI

to be stored or dried, however, are better harvested around a new moon. The medicinal properties of plants are said to be most concentrated during the period of the waning moon, so this is the best time to harvest herbs for medicinal use.

Some lunar gardening systems place more emphasis on the ascending and descending moon, linking the rise and fall of sap within plants to this cycle instead. According to this system, when the moon is ascending, sap rises and energy is concentrated in the parts of plants above ground. When the moon is descending, energies are drawn into the parts of plants below ground. Clearly, since the waxing/waning and ascending/descending cycles are of slightly different lengths and so are rarely synchronised, a choice has to be made here; it is difficult to take account of both.

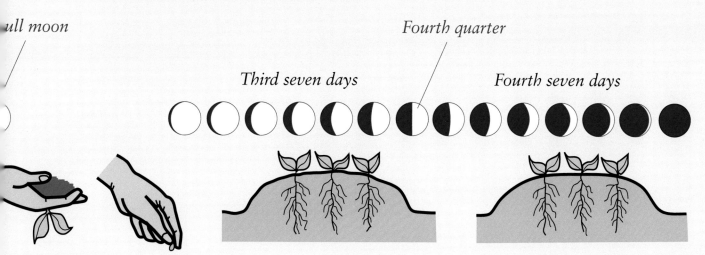

ull moon

Fourth quarter

Third seven days

Fourth seven days

splant seedlings into trays and plant
-germinating seeds (most flowers)
trays and/or beds

Increased root growth rate

Balanced decrease in rate of root and leaf growth (resting period)

MOONLIGHT DECREASING
LUNAR GRAVITY DECREASING

MOONLIGHT DECREASING
LUNAR GRAVITY INCREASING

Planting by the sidereal cycle

The waxing/waning cycle relates mostly to general plant growth; it is the sidereal cycle, which relates principally to the moment of sowing, that has most significance for crop yield and keeping quality. It is therefore important that sowings are made while the moon is passing through a constellation relating to the appropriate element – an earth constellation for potatoes, for instance, and a water constellation for lettuces.

The optimum time to sow is as near to the centre of an appropriate constellation as possible – or, some authorities suggest, just as the moon enters the constellation, so that the sowing has two full days under the auspices of the appropriate element. You should avoid sowing just before the moon moves out of a constellation. The moon returns to the same element every nine days, so if weather or competing commitments mean that you miss one sowing opportunity, waiting until the next will not involve too much of a delay.

Some authorities, including biodynamists, believe that all work with plants should be carried out under the appropriate moon-sign element. Carrots, for instance, should be thinned, weeded and watered on a root day; this enhances the positive effect of sowing them at the right time. Each time you cultivate a plant, you moderate or reinforce the influences set in train at sowing time. If you have sown a crop at an unfavourable time, you can mitigate that to a degree by cultivating it at a favourable time.

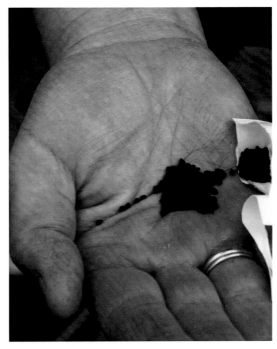

The sidereal cycle relates principally to the moment of sowing. Picture: Dave Bevan

The planting of fruit trees and bushes should be done when the moon is passing through a fire constellation, and ideally you should also take advantage of a favourable moon/Saturn aspect. These plants are long-term additions to your garden, so it makes even more sense to pick the most favourable day for planting.

Less emphasis is placed on harvesting crops under an appropriate moon-sign, but there are times when it is relevant. Fruits and vegetables that do not store well will last much longer if you avoid harvesting them on water days. Making jams and jellies and bottling and freezing fruit is best done on a fire/warmth day. If you want to save your own seed to sow next year, that should be done on a day appropriate to the kind of plant.

Planting on an appropriate day is particularly important with long-term additions to the garden like fruit trees; heel them in and wait for an auspicious day if necessary. Picture: Dave Bevan

8 | HOW TO USE THE MOON CALENDAR

Planting by the moon involves taking account of a whole range of interlocking – and sometimes conflicting – cycles and events, and the first tool a prospective lunar gardener needs is a moon planting calendar. This will present all the information in an accessible visual format, noting the moon's position in the waxing/waning and ascending/descending cycles, its apogee and perigee, special events like nodes, eclipses and aspects, and whether the moon is in an earth, water, air or fire constellation.

The symbols used in planting calendars can be confusing at first, but they will become familiar with use. The information they convey will let you make an informed decision about what gardening tasks are most appropriate to the day – or whether gardening is appropriate at all. There are one or two days in every month where the influences are sufficiently negative that it is advised that you simply stay out of the garden.

Right: Sample page from Michael Littlewood's Gardening by the Moon Calendar, available from www.ecodesignscape.co.uk

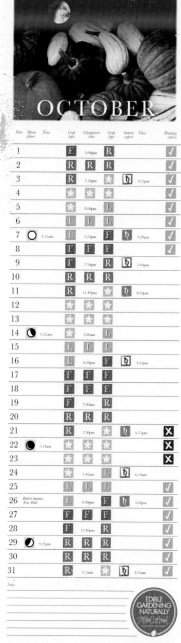

The quantity of information can still be overwhelming, and it is useful simply to begin with observation. Refer to your calendar, take note of where the moon is in its various cycles and whether it is a root, leaf, flower or fruit/seed day, and observe how your plants respond to the different energy cycles. Then, when you are ready, start to put lunar gardening into practice. If it is a root day, plant potatoes, or thin carrots; if it is a leaf day, sow salad crops or transplant cabbages. If your gardening year is underway and your seeds are already in the ground, introduce gardening by the moon at whatever point your plants have reached; it will all be beneficial.

Once you become accustomed to this way of gardening, it is not difficult to accommodate the advice of a lunar planting calendar and tailor the work you do accordingly. It should be said, however, that moon gardening is not really compatible with sporadic gardening. If, for instance, you can only get into your garden at the weekend, it is going to be very difficult to schedule work with your crops for the appropriate time. Working with a lunar calendar is really only feasible if you are able to work in your garden at least every other day, so that you can undertake any necessary work with root, leaf, flower and fruit/seed crops within each nine-day cycle.

Moon gardening is also not compatible with disorganised gardening. Planning ahead is important; if, for example, you want to plant your potatoes at a particular time, it is essential that you have seed tubers, compost and tools to hand when the moon enters the earth sign closest to that date.

Work with potatoes should be undertaken on a root day. Picture: Dave Bevan

Be aware, however, that the advice offered in lunar planting guides is sometimes idealistic to the point of being impractical. For instance, one book suggests that in wet weather you should hoe in the morning in a fire or air sign when the moon is waning. This implies a period of some 17 consecutive days when hoeing is not advisable – which would result in a major weed problem. There are instances where the best time to do a job is when it needs doing, irrespective of the moon.

It is important to temper lunar planting with common sense, and to remember that a planting calendar is a guide, not a straightjacket. You need to factor in other things, such as the weather. There is no point, for instance, in sowing seeds at full moon if the ground is frozen or waterlogged that week. The principle that they will germinate best at this time only holds if other factors are favourable.

Remember that your own powers of observation are as important a guide as any calendar – and that they will become more honed as you become more familiar with this method. Gardening, particularly organic and biodynamic gardening, is very specific to your own individual patch of land, and you will find that you become the best judge of what will work for you. As you become more confident in this way of gardening, you may wish to conduct your own experiments – sowing at new moon and again at full moon, for instance, and comparing the results.

The Biodynamic Garden at Garden Organic Ryton in Warwickshire. Picture: Michael Littlewood

9 | CONCLUSION

To acknowledge the cycles of the heavens, known and worked with for thousands of years, is to begin to understand our gardens' relationship to the earth and the skies. Working with the patterns of the moon as well as the sun offers us a simple way of making the most of our outdoor space. But although gardening by the moon draws upon wisdom stretching back millennia, it is still a new science. We do not have the whole picture yet, which is one of the reasons there are so many conflicting opinions. It is therefore all the more important that we become our own experts, testing what we read and observing the results in our own garden.

The rewards are immense. As we learn to attune our gardening to the cycles of the moon and the planets, we can expect increasingly reliable germination of seeds, healthier, more vibrant plant growth, and more vital, nutritious and productive crops – and our experience of gardening will become ever more fulfilling, and more enjoyable.

Picture opposite: Dave Bevan

Further reading

Enchanted Garden Cuthbertson, Tom (Rider & Co/Hutchinson, 1979)
How to Grow More Vegetables Jeavons, John (Ten Speed Press, 1982; revised edition 2006)
Gardening and Planting by the Moon Kollerstrom, Nick (Quantum, published annually)
Moon Time Paungger, Johanna & Poppe, Thomas (C W Daniel Co, 1999)
The Art of Timing: The Application of Lunar Cycles in Daily Life Paungger, Johanna & Poppe, Thomas
    (C W Daniel Co, 2000)
Astrological Gardening Riotte, Louise (Wings Books, 2002)
Stella Natura (Biodynamic Agricultural Centre, published annually)
Work on the Land and the Constellations Thun, Maria (The Landthorn Press, 1979)
Biodynamic Gardening for Health and Taste Wright, Hilary (Floris Books, 2003; paperback edition 2009)
www.considera.org   Website collating experimental lunar planting results
www.plantingbythemoon.co.uk

Acknowledgments

*I am very grateful to the following people who helped to make this publication possible but my thanks go especially to **Gaby Bartai** for her writing and editing and to **Andrew Crane** for his layout and graphics.*

*Thanks to **Sally Cunningham** and **Elspeth Thompson** for reading the manuscript so willingly and promptly.*
*Thanks also to **Garden Organic** for allowing me to take photographs of the Biodynamic Garden.*
*Thanks also to **Cockington Court Kitchen Garden** for allowing use of their photographs.*

*I also thank **Sally Cunningham** for sending so many wonderful images for us to use*
*and **Dave Bevan** for the images from his very extensive library.*

*Thanks too, to **Mike Hedges** and **Indra Starnes** of **Chase Organics**, for their support and encouragement.*

Publications by Michael Littlewood

Gardening Calendars
Gardening by the Moon Calendar (annual)
Gardener's Monthly Reminder Calendar (perpetual)
Seasonal Availability Calendar (perpetual)

Gardening Charts
Companion Planting Chart
Vegetable Planning Chart
Vegetable Growing Chart

Gardening Books
The Organic Gardener's Handbook (Crowood Press, 2007)
A Guide to Companion Planting (Michael Littlewood, 2009)

See www.ecodesignscape.co.uk for full details and images.

Useful contacts

Biodynamic Agriculture Association (BDAA)
Painswick Inn Project
Gloucester Street, Stroud
GL5 1QG

Tel: 01453 759501
Email: bdaa@biodynamic.org.uk
Web: www.biodynamic.org.uk

Garden Organic
Ryton, Coventry
CV8 3LG

Tel: 024 7630 8210
Email: enquiry@gardenorganic.org.uk
Web: www.gardenorganic.org.uk

Chase Organics Ltd
Heritage House
52-54 Hamm Moor Lane
Addlestone, Surrey
KT15 2SF

Tel: 01932 878570

Email: enquiries@chaseorganics.co.uk
Web: www.OrganicCatalogue.com